JE
Mara, Wil.
Quite enough hot dogs

A Rookie reader

Quite Enough Hot Dogs

Written by Wil Mara
Illustrated by Pete Whitehead

Children's Press
An Imprint of Scholastic Inc.
New York • Toronto • London • Auckland • Sydney
Mexico City • New Delhi • Hong Kong
Danbury, Connecticut

To my mom, who always said this would happen.
—W. P. M.

To Bailey and Chelsea—No hot dog has a chance
with them in the room.
—P. W.

Reading Consultant

Cecilia Minden-Cupp, PhD
Former Director of the Language and Literacy Program
Harvard Graduate School of Education
Cambridge, Massachusetts

Cover design: The Design Lab
Interior design: Herman Adler

Library of Congress Cataloging-in-Publication Data

Mara, Wil.
  Quite enough hot dogs / by Wil Mara; illustrated by Pete Whitehead.
    p. cm. — (Rookie reader: silent letters)
  ISBN-13: 978-0-531-17548-4 (lib. bdg.)   978-0-531-17782-2 (pbk.)
  ISBN-10: 0-531-17548-0 (lib. bdg.)   0-531-17782-3 (pbk.)
  1. English language—Consonants—Juvenile literature. 2. English
language—Vowels—Juvenile literature. I. Whitehead, Peter, ill.
II. Title. III. Series.
  PE1159.M37 2007
  428.1'3—dc22   2006024391

"What can I eat?" asked Steve.
"I know! Please make one more hot dog!"

3

"Ugh," said Mom. "You are going to turn into a huge hot dog!" Steve laughed and took another bite.

But Steve's stomach ached
after eating all those hot dogs.
He decided to sleep for a while.

When Steve woke, he could
smell the scent of hot dogs.
Mmmmm . . .

But he could not get up!
Steve fell to the floor.

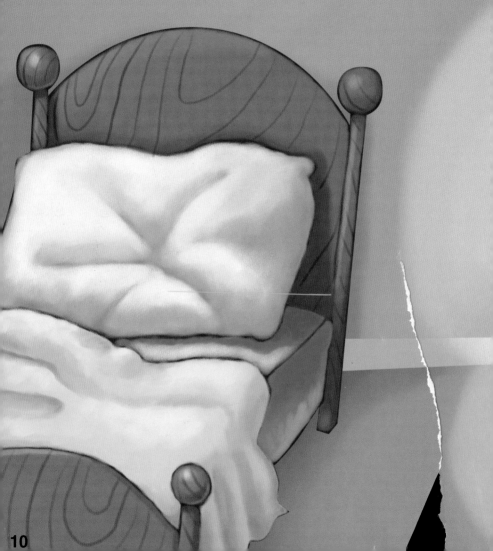

He faced the mirror.
Eek! Steve had turned into a hot dog!

"Mom! Something is quite wrong!"
Steve cried tears of yellow mustard.

He wiggled down the stairs.
"Mom! Help!"

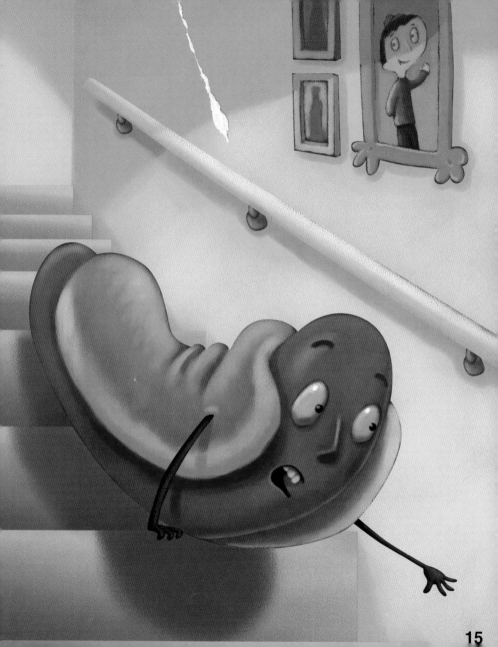

15

Mom wasn't there, but
someone else was.

It was Steve's dog Nate.
Nate loved hot dogs, too!

Nate wagged his tail.
"No, Nate, no!" Steve cried.
Nate ran after him.

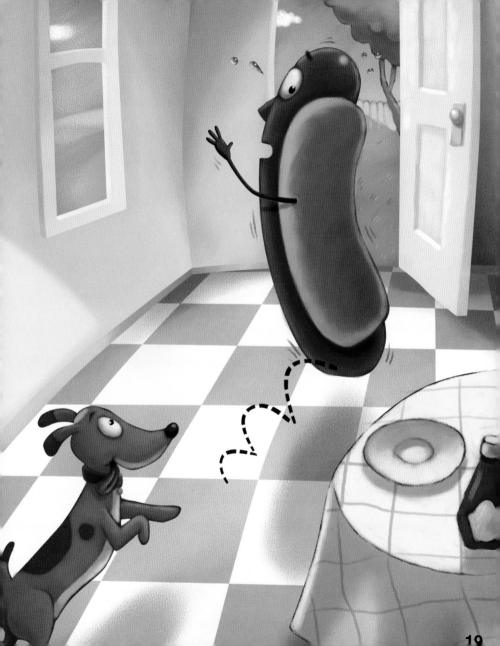

Steve made his way to the backyard,
but Nate chased him.

Steve couldn't escape!
Nate leapt into the air
with his mouth wide open.

23

"No!" Steve screamed.
But just before Nate took
a bite, Steve woke up.

25

Steve raced to the mirror.
Now he knew it had all been a dream!

Steve went down to the kitchen.
"What about another hot dog?"
asked Mom. "No!" Steve answered.

"But I thought you liked hot dogs!"

"I guess I changed my mind!"

Word list (118 words)

(Words in **bold** have the silent e sound.)

a	down	is	of	thought
about	dream	it	one	to
ached	eat	just	open	too
after	eating	kitchen	**please**	took
air	eek	knew	**quite**	turn
all	else	know	**raced**	turned
and	**escape**	laughed	ran	ugh
another	**faced**	leapt	said	up
answered	fell	**liked**	scent	wagged
are	floor	loved	screamed	was
asked	for	**made**	sleep	wasn't
backyard	get	**make**	smell	way
been	going	mind	smell	went
before	guess	mirror	someone	what
bite	had	mmmmm	something	when
but	he	Mom	stairs	**while**
can	help	more	**Steve**	**wide**
changed	him	mouth	**Steve's**	wiggled
chased	his	mustard	stomach	with
could	hot dog	my	tail	**woke**
couldn't	hot dogs	**Nate**	tears	wrong
cried	**huge**	no	the	yellow
decided	I	not	there	you
dog	into	now	**those**	

About the Author

Wil Mara has written more than seventy books, many of which are educational titles for young readers.

About the Illustrator

Pete Whitehead has been an amateur hot dog eater since he was three years old. He prefers mustard to ketchup and would never say no to sauerkraut. When not eating hot dogs, he spends a lot of time drawing and looking forward to his next hot dog.